THE MADNESS WITHIN

My Struggle With Manic Depression

Cheryl G. Baker

authorHOUSE®

AuthorHouse™
1663 Liberty Drive, Suite 200
Bloomington, IN 47403
www.authorhouse.com
Phone: 1-800-839-8640

First published by AuthorHouse   4/9/2009

ISBN: 978-1-4389-6269-6 (sc)

Printed in the United States of America
Bloomington, Indiana

This book is printed on acid-free paper.

DEDICATION

I would like to dedicate *The Madness Within* to my husband, John, for understanding, supporting, defending and most of all loving me throughout my everlasting journey with Bipolar Disorder since the beginning of my relationship with him.

I would also like to dedicate this book to my entire family, including my Aunt, for helping me through all of my hard times and providing me with unconditional love.

Thank you Mom and Dad for raising me in a Christian home which provided me with the foundation I needed for spiritual growth.

INTRODUCTION

Sometimes it is hard to accept the fact that I suffer from Bipolar Disorder. I often look at others (assuming they are free of the illness) wishing that I could be like them. In fact it is almost a daily occurrence. But, I go on and try not to concentrate on it, because the illness only gets worse. I feel the need to reach out to others that are affected by Bipolar Disorder just to encourage them that there is hope.

In writing this book, I put the use of my knowledge and experiences to help others identify and obtain treatment in order to have the best quality of life possible. For some life may overall be very satisfying, for others struggling to achieve stability is a lifelong process.

I struggle every day of my life, but I know I will be all right because I have found peace with God.

CONTENTS

CHAPTER 1

MANIC—DEPRESSION 101

Welcome to Manic-Depression 101.
Before I begin to tell my story about my lifelong
struggle with Manic-Depression, also known as
Bipolar Disorder, there are some facts you need to
know in regards to this mental illness. You will
probably find that you know someone, whether it
is a family member, a friend or perhaps yourself,
who suffers from this serious condition.

In this first chapter, the information provided
for you will assist you in identifying and
understanding Manic-Depression. I also hope
it will help clarify any misconceptions you may
have. Not only will it allow you to become more
knowledgeable about this subject matter, it will
also hopefully enable you to be more objective,
tolerant and less judgmental of individuals afflicted

with this illness. You will learn how devastating Manic-Depression can be and see what is meant by a real "roller-coaster ride" that is, unfortunately, not in a theme park.

Individuals who suffer with Manic-Depression live very tumultuous lives. There are different types and various degrees of the illness which fall on a wide spectrum ranging from depression to euphoria. Everyone is unique and experiences various symptoms. While many individuals live very productive lives, others are more dysfunctional. Much of this may depend on the response to medication, treatment, and the severity of the illness.

The following information needed to describe symptoms of Manic-Depression was gathered from Kaplan and Sadock's *Synopsis of Psychiatry* (8th edition).

Manic-Depression is a mood disorder caused by a chemical imbalance in the brain. It is believed that genetic, biochemical and environmental factors contribute to the cause and effect of the illness. It is often exacerbated by distressing events. While most people experience a normal range of ups and downs, Manic-Depressives experience extreme mood swings that may last in duration. A delay in diagnosis and treatment could potentially lead to suicide. Even if treated, there are some risks.

Mania is characterized by a heightened mood, an inflated self-esteem and a feeling of self-importance. Persons feel overly optimistic and very confident. They are known to be "on top of the world," can be very amusing and are "the life of the party." There is an increase in mental and physical activity. Racing thoughts jump from one subject to another very quickly. Speech becomes rapid, loud and increases as the mania intensifies. Reckless behavior and erratic driving are also typical of Manic-Depression. During some episodes, shopping sprees are common often resulting in financial difficulties for family members.

Moods swing from euphoria to depression and are often accompanied by irritability and agitation. Moods shift from minutes to hours. Sleep deprivation during a manic phase is also common. Talking on the phone during early hours of the morning is typical of Manic-Depressives often disturbing others trying to sleep. Manic individuals exhibit signs of sexual indiscretion, poor judgment and poor impulse control. They can be assaultive, threatening to others and may break laws. Grandiose delusions and hallucinations are present at times during episodes. In more serious cases, individuals may play with their feces and drink their urine.

Opposite of mania is depression. A prolonged depressed mood and a loss of interest or pleasure are symptomatic of depression and are distinctly different from normal emotions during grief or sadness. Patients with depression describe it as having agonizing pain.

Some patients have significant changes in sleeping patterns and appetite. Patients can be agitated, angry, pessimistic, hopeless, and lethargic at times. Marked anxiety often accompanies a depressed episode. Depressed individuals develop feelings of guilt, worthlessness and a loss of energy. Inability to concentrate, enjoy former interests and social withdrawals are also key factors. Trouble performing sexual activity is very common.

Studies indicate that two-thirds of the patients with severe depression contemplate suicide. Up to twenty per cent actually do commit suicide. However, studies show that eighty per cent of depressed individuals who receive proper treatment show significant improvement and lead relatively productive lives.

CHAPTER 2

SMILE IT'S NOT THAT BAD

At times I feel reluctant to talk about my mental illness because of the stigma that goes along with it. I believe that society dictates the perception amongst many people to believe the brain is a separate entity detached from the rest of the human body. Diabetes, alcoholism or heart disease, for example, are more acceptable conditions than Manic Depression.

Mentally ill individuals are often ostracized by others and are believed to be "crazy" or "sick in the head." A great number of those people have yet to be diagnosed because they may refuse to see that they have a problem themselves. For example, in many instances, alcoholics only mask their problems by self-medicating with the use of alcohol. Which is worse, not seeking the help needed or addressing the problem and receiving proper treatment?

No, I'm not a rich or famous person who is known throughout the world. If I were famous, many people would read this autobiography due to the publicity it would receive. Even the most ludicrous articles in tabloids about famous people draw a great deal of attention. I am an ordinary dysfunctional person who suffers from a serious and debilitating mental illness. I guess it may be less interesting to read an autobiography about someone you have never heard of; however, I would like to tell my story in hopes that I may lead individuals needing treatment to seek help.

I have been diagnosed with Manic-Depression, and to put it bluntly, if another person approaches me one more time and says, "smile, it's not all that bad," I think I will scream! That statement is very annoying to me because many times **it is all that bad.** Realistically someone could be going through a major crisis in their life, or in my case I may be experiencing a severe Manic-Depressive episode. So, if you are a "smile, it's not all that bad" person, you might want to think twice before you say it again.

Persons suffering from Manic-Depression (bipolar disorder) display their outward expressions which reflect their inward feelings and emotions. It is extremely difficult to mask what lies beneath. Others who are not bipolar have less difficulty camouflaging their inward feelings which can be advantageous in certain situations.

I once read an article in a publication describing Manic-Depression. It wasn't quite worded this way but I will paraphrase it to the best of my knowledge. It basically read, **normalcy is a place you visit, not a residence.** I had never heard it put that way before; however, it is as close to the truth as you can get.

In the next several chapters I will describe to you how Manic-Depression has affected my life. It has had an enormous negative impact. My actual diagnosis is "Mixed Bipolar Disorder," meaning the illness manifests itself by highs and lows frequently occurring simultaneously in nature but not always. Sometimes I have full-fledged manic episodes and other times debilitating depressions. I taped many of my episodes from November 2002 through August 2005 that will hopefully express my feelings in words you can understand. I will begin by describing a slightly manic episode which lasted approximately one week in duration. Following this episode I have written from an actual recording of a mixed episode which may be difficult to follow; however, I will explain what actually transpired. Next I will write from an actual recording of a short but severe anxiety episode that I experienced which was accompanied by a deep underlying depression. Finally I will describe another brief manic episode with borderline clinical features of psychosis. Before I begin to describe some of my episodes, there were a few extraneous conditions that I was living with that need to be addressed.

CHAPTER 3

GLAD, SAD AND MAD

EPISODE 1

It was a Monday morning. The air was crisp and cool. The clouds were very ominous looking as though it would storm any minute. I went outside to get a breath of fresh air. I felt relatively happy, but there was an underlying feeling of sadness within me. At the time, I was bombarded with a series of stressors which exacerbated my mental condition. My husband and I were facing financial difficulties. We live on one income, with the exception of the monthly disability check I receive, which provides very little additional income. Bills were piling high and we often didn't know whether we would make it from week to week. Sometimes we were so inundated with bills we had to rely on my parents to bail us out in order to make ends meet.

In addition, I had numerous medical problems resulting in many doctors' visits and hospitalizations. I had been diagnosed with Spinal Arthritis which affected my entire body leaving me in agonizing pain. All of the physical activities that I took for granted were no longer an option for me. Every single morning when I woke up I could barely walk and this made me more depressed than I already was.

Within a year, I found out that my thyroid gland wasn't functioning and I had gained 60 lbs. which naturally affected my self-image. I also learned that I had high blood, very high Triglycerides and cholesterol as well as pre-diabetes (which was later found inaccurate). And to top it all, I was in menopause! I smoked incessantly and learned that I had the beginning stages of emphysema.

If that wasn't enough, after several sessions with my mental health therapist it was concluded, although without any clear evidence, that I suffered from Disassociative Disorder resulting from an assumed traumatic event which happened earlier in my childhood years. This was so alarming to me that I discontinued treatment because of the mental anguish it created and the depressive effect at the end of each session as well as my disbelief in the diagnosis. I felt as if a diagnosis was being forced upon me which created a lot of confusion. In retrospect I believe the diagnosis was fabricated in order to correspond to psychological science, but it was unclear.

As a result I was fat, I was discouraged, and my self-esteem was low----not low, but extremely low when adding Manic-Depression into the equation. Just knowing I am Bipolar is a main stressor itself because of the rapid cycles of mania and depression leaving me clueless as to how I will feel minute to minute.

Not only did I feel like a hopeless case at times, I developed a fear of socializing with others because of my insecurities, my very low self-esteem and my inferiority to others. I was conditioning myself to become a recluse as I preferred to stay at home where I felt safe.

I created an enmeshed relationship with my parents as a result of my mental condition. They were beyond being a support system for me to rely on. I placed them in the position of dictating almost every decision I made. Clearly I would like to be more autonomous but due to the severity of my illness, it is very difficult.

Some people who know me well believe my disorder has made it easier for me to inadvertently use my illness as a crutch to avoid confronting and solving unpleasant or difficult situations on my own as well as avoiding other responsibilities I may have. As a result, I become very annoyed with those who have these beliefs because I know that this is not true.

Finally, I was living in confusion as I shifted from one belief system to another (morally and spiritually). Unfortunately there were a lot of extraneous circumstances that I was facing and still face in my life today.

Recognizing that I had confused feelings of happiness and sadness, I was fortunate to have an appointment that day to see my psychiatrist as my sadness could have spiraled into a debilitating depression causing me to have suicidal thoughts. Upon arrival for my visit with my psychiatrist, I asked her to please do something to take my sadness away.

At the time I was taking three mood stabilizers, two antidepressants, an antipsychotic and medication for anxiety, not to mention all of the medication I was taking for my medical problems. I was taking more than 25 pills per day. I felt like a drug addict----you know, a pill popping bitch!

The anti-psychotic medication I was taking caused me to sleep walk. As I walked I would bump into walls as if I were drunk, causing injury to myself. I would also doze off with lit cigarettes in my hand or mouth or at times when I was eating. Fortunately I never caught myself or anything around me on fire or choked myself to death.

I developed an addiction to Xanax (used for anxiety) which many physicians hesitate to prescribe because of that very reason. I began abusing the drug because as time went on, it didn't provide me with the same effect as it previously had. I used the drug to numb myself to the least little thing that made me nervous. I couldn't handle any stimuli and I just wanted to remain calm and laid back without a care in the world. I informed my psychiatrist about my addiction because I was concerned. We made a verbal contract for me to stop over-using the medication or I would have to discontinue using the drug altogether. In an attempt to alleviate my sadness, my psychiatrist increased one of my anti-depressants (Zoloft) and insisted that I contact her in the event that I should become manic.

Following my psychiatric visit I had already begun noticing a change in my mood and gradually became more manic as the days progressed.

Cognitively I knew what was happening to me, but I couldn't control it. My husband said that he liked my manic state, probably because I had been depressed for the last several months. He described me as being fun and amusing. In my opinion I was totally out of control and acted like an idiot! Individuals have told me they wish they could experience mania, but in my case that's a joke. I tend to get in trouble with my mouth during a manic phase. In any case, I became so wired I felt like I was on speed. I paced the floors so quickly my dogs even looked at me as if I were crazy. Later, I began to act impulsively as I went on shopping sprees spending money on items I really couldn't afford. My judgment was impaired and my speech became rapid. My mania became so problematic that I began to stutter. I usually become obnoxious by acting in ways and saying things I often regret, and I often get on my own nerves. Fortunately, I didn't become obnoxious this time..

I decided to contact my doctor for an emergency appointment fearing the escalation of the mania. On the way there I was so paranoid that I was afraid I would wreck the car. I had already been in three accidents within a six-month period and driving became a fear to me altogether. My arms were shaking as I gripped the steering wheel. I didn't know how I could possibly make it there and back. When I finally reached my destination, my psychiatrist evaluated me and insisted that I discontinue taking the Zoloft. When I left her office, I actually got lost on the way home on a road I traveled frequently. I panicked but eventually found my way back home. I stopped taking the Zoloft and within a few days I was stabilized.

In this incident, I didn't allow my manic state to escalate unlike some other incidents that I will share with you later. I have a Master's Degree in Social Work and therefore, I often use my training ability to analyze what is happening to me. Fortunately I know when to seek help. I was told by two previous psychiatrists, after telling them about my Master's in Social Work, that a little bit of knowledge can get you in a lot of trouble. In return, at the risk of sounding cocky, I responded, "a lot of knowledge isn't worth anything if you don't know how to successfully treat your patients" (as you will observe in one of the following chapters entitled Dr. Doo Little).

My next episode was taken from an actual recording. Some of the material was omitted due to the content and offensive language, however part of this material was not omitted so that readers will be made aware of the behavioral changes during each episode.

EPISODE 2

"It's November 23, 2002 at 1:30 in the afternoon. I'm trying to calm my ass down. I've had a really screwed up day! I woke up at 5 a.m. and I was okay. I woke my husband up, fixed his coffee and sent him off to work. I started crying, but I don't know why. I guess I was sad because he had to work overtime today and it's the weekend. We really need the money, but I miss him. I cried about three hours this morning. I feel like I have literally been beaten.

My brother and his wife recently decided to end their marriage, and when I found out the news I was devastated. I'm very close to my brother and sister, and anything that affects them affects me a great deal. I was so sad that I called my mom. She tried to calm me down, and told me to take a step backward and not to get so involved in my brother's life. I took her advice and found things to keep me occupied. I was so down I decided to write in my journal. I began writing about the things I was thinking about, especially suicide. If something ever happens to my husband I will kill myself because I can't live without him. If I do commit suicide, I have it all planned out. It's pretty sick thinking but people don't understand my illness and the circumstances I live with. I can't work so how can I support myself. I have no children to love and to live for. My husband is my life and the only thing I have. If he's gone, I'm going right behind him. I've always got that in the back of my mind. Even when I'm happy, I have it in the back of my mind. I snapped out of it later this morning, so I fixed myself a cup of coffee. I started feeling better so I went to the bank, ran some errands and out of nowhere I was driving down the road and the car in front of me kept slowing down, putting on the brakes and I got mad as shit. I yelled, 'what the f— is your problem? Get the hell out of my way!' So I swerved around him, moved in front of him and slammed on the brakes. I said, 'how do you like that mother f-----, how do you like that?' So they backed off. I mean I was hot. I was really hot under the collar and I just couldn't quit cussing. I just lost complete control of myself and I could not believe what was happening to me. Evidently the people in the other car got pissed off as they pulled up beside me. It was two men . It looked like they said 'what the f— is your problem.' So I just shot them the bird and said 'f---- you! I thought they were going to follow me. I was scared but I was in 'road rage!' I sped off and lost them, Thank God! My moods have been rapidly shifting up and down this morning and I don't understand what is happening to me. I quickly went from sad to mad. I feel like I'm losing my mind!

Right now I am thinking clearly, but 30 minutes ago I was wild. 'Let me tell you something, I am one psychotic bitch, and I don't know why my husband stays with me.' This house (pacing the floor) is a f------ wreck. I can't keep the house clean. Oh great, here is another pee stain. It is either Spunky's or Buffy's (dogs) mess. I've got no motivation to clean or do anything. I don't know whether I'm depressed or just lazy. I need someone to whip my ass or at least shake me in order to put some sense into me. 'F— you mother f-------'(referring to me) (Crash!) I threw the phone across the room. 'Spunky, I'm sorry...I'm not going to hurt you'. He's hiding under the kitchen table because he is scared of me. 'Help me.' (Screaming desperately for help from anyone, but particularly from God.) 'I want to be a good wife, but I'm not.' Buffy is just laying there. She is just chilling out. She's not even scared of me. Why not? She should be the one raising hell. She is the one who is pregnant. 'Help me God. (screaming and crying) Why do I have to live like this? After experiencing this episode I became very depressed. I went to bed."

"It's Sunday, November 24 at 8:30 a.m. Today I am finally stabilized. Now that I am able to think clearly, I can explain what happened. I vacillated between agitation with aggression and depression. I experienced extreme agitation while hurling myself into a road rage. When I returned home after the incident, I thought I was stable and began putting my episode on tape. Obviously I wasn't stable as I became quite upset again. I became verbally offensive again as I often do when I become unstable. I spoke of suicide because I have a fear of abandonment and feel I cannot live without my husband. I feel I have nothing to live for so why hang around. Again, even though I have a Master's Degree in Social Work, I can't work, I can't have children, I'm emotionally and mentally disabled and I don't bring in enough disability to take care of myself. I have my family but it's different from having your own nuclear family. I've talked to numerous therapists about this issue but it never gets addressed much less resolved. People say taking your own life will surely send you into the gates of hell. Even if I do go to hell, at desperate times I really don't care because I already live in hell. I couldn't believe I had recorded this episode on tape. I felt like a newscaster recording a live hurricane on CNN, only I was the hurricane."

"On November 29, only a few days later, I was in a car accident and the other driver was at fault. A female police officer arrived while I was in the process of cursing at the other driver. The police officer threatened to arrest me if I didn't quit using profanity. Again I was in an uncontrollable rage. At a later date following this incident, I was admitted to a psychiatric facility for a medication adjustment and was advised to participate in an Anger Management Class. I didn't see why I needed to attend the class at this time. However, soon after class began a small woman came up to me and confronted me while I was seated. She threatened me and wanted to have a fist fight. Her size wasn't a deterrent from engaging in such a ludicrous act. I began laughing at her as she screamed obscenities at me. Although we never fought, only because I was twice her size and the fact that I wanted to save myself from embarrassment, I felt extremely provoked and didn't want to injure her too badly.

In retrospect, excluding this particular case, it seems as the years have passed I have become less fearful of others but more apt to be confrontational. It is probably due to the increasing anger I feel inside. In this case it was certainly ironic that the facilitator, who was a mental health practitioner, had no idea how to handle this particular situation even though it was an Anger Management Class. Eventually the woman stopped fussing on her own and took a seat."

Episode 3
(Anxiety Attack)

"It's January 26, 2003. I'm having an anxiety attack. I'm scared of being me. I'm scared of being a Manic-Depressive. I'm scared of living. I'm scared of dying. I'm scared my husband is going to die before I do and I will have to kill myself. I pray that God will take me first so I won't have to tolerate the pain of being left behind. I feel trapped. I want to live, but I don't want to live. I'm scared to die, but I've tried to take my life twice. I hate myself and my life. It's not fair. Why can't I be an ordinary person. It's horrible that there are times I want to end my life." (End of recording.)

I can recall being scared of stability at times, because I never have really known how it feels over any length of time. At times stability is an uncomfortable feeling because I know my mood will not last long and I'm always anticipating the swing itself. If I'm contemplating my mood swinging back down, I'm not free of anxiety because swinging down is one of my fears.

Therefore, I'm not as stable as I thought to begin with. It is a vicious, perpetual cycle and a "no- win" situation. Anyone who has ever experienced anxiety knows it is a terrible feeling. Individuals suffering from anxiety experience it for various reasons and sometimes it's origin is hard to identify. My biggest fear is abandonment. My fear of social involvement with others has evolved into a social phobia. It's not uncommon to have some anxieties and not all need to be treated with medication. However, the more severe cases, such as mine, definitely deserve some attention.

I remember recording this episode in the back bedroom while sitting on the bed. I remember whispering everything I said so my husband wouldn't hear me. I try to keep as many episodes as I possibly can to myself. I don't want to drive my husband away although he says I never will. In any event, I don't want to risk losing him. If he only knew how depressed I feel every single morning that I wake up and how scared I am of myself because of my suicidal thoughts when he leaves for work."

Episode 4
(Mania with Possible Psychosis)

"One summer night in June, 2004, my husband and I and another couple went to a bar on karaoke night. I hadn't been drinking, but then again I don't have to drink to have fun.

I sang my favorite tune (Black Velvet) as if I were a pop star. That is the only song I can sing well. In fact, that is the only song I will sing in any karaoke bar. I must have done a pretty good job because the DJ threw a dollar bill on the floor in front of me. After I finished singing, I didn't want to leave the stage because I was having so much fun and enjoying the attention—so I stayed. But, this time was different from any other time I had performed. I was in a daze. It seemed like the room was full of smoke and I could hardly make anyone out in the audience. All of a sudden I started acting as though I was a comedian. I felt so elated. Without realizing what I was doing, I began to talk about sex and began to make racial slurs. I noticed a couple of girls at the bar in the back, one who was a so-called friend of mine, making comments about me. Who could blame them. I'm sure that if I witnessed another female who was saying the things I said, I might become judgmental towards her as well.

Although my husband thought I was hilarious, he was afraid of what might come out of my mouth next. So he literally dragged me off the stage.

CHAPTER 4

OH GOD, PLEASE FORGIVE ME

I WAS diagnosed with Bipolar Disorder at the age of eighteen; however, I question whether it began during my earlier stages of development. I can remember as far back as five years old, when I experienced night terrors. I distinctly remember having repetitive dreams of an unexplainable heavy force (my parents told me I sometimes called it a truck) falling on me. I would scream and go into such a deep trance from which my parents could not awake me. They would try to calm me down by holding me and talking to me. Eventually when I became calm, I would return to a peaceful sleep.

My parents described me as a very happy child with a bubbly personality. Little did they know I experienced a lot of anxiety. I didn't enjoy school because I felt uncomfortable and nervous, and did not feel secure. Although I made lots of friends and I did well academically, it still gave me an unsettled feeling. When I was in the second grade I remember sitting at my desk in class, and every time I swallowed I felt something go down my throat. I thought I was swallowing my brains! I didn't reveal this to anyone even though it was a petrifying experience. I actually thought I was dying! It began happening on a daily basis but eventually stopped.

I was raised with a Christian background, Baptist to be more specific. I attended church regularly and made God a very significant part of my life. In fact, I became a Christian at the early age of eight.

I was overweight as a child and often teased by others. I was recognized as "the blow toad" by my family members as a joke resulting from a T-shirt I wore with the emblem of a toad across my chest. I also went fishing with my father on our summer vacation in Nag's Head, North Carolina, and I caught my first fish. It was a blow toad. It was inevitable that, since my cheeks were so puffy and I was as big as a blimp, the name would stick with me. But, it gets worse. The nickname "blow toad" evolved into the new nickname "two-ton toad" as I got bigger. Now that hurt! I never overindulged in the consumption of food. I just had prolonged baby fat, if that is any consolation. When I asked my Mother if she thought I was fat, she would reply, "no, you are just pleasantly plump," being the kind of Mother she is. I believed her then, but now looking back I realize I was a porker. I felt so ashamed that I tore up most of my childhood pictures.

I became interested in boys as early as kindergarten. I can remember my 3rd Grade boyfriend telling someone, as I eavesdropped, "I don't care if she's fat, I still like her." Although it was awfully kind of him to say, it left a bitter sweet taste in my mouth. This same boyfriend chased me behind a tree in elementary school because he wanted to kiss me. I remember holding out my arm to let him kiss my hand instead of my lips. He lived in my neighborhood and on numerous occasions he wanted me to come over after school. I was afraid of what he might want to do, so each time he asked, I would tell him I had to go to the dentist. That excuse got old quickly, but I continued to use it whenever he popped the question.

I was a well-behaved child-----at least until I went to church. I would sit up in the balcony with my friends, make spit balls and flick them off of the balcony so that they would land in the old ladies' hairdos. It seemed so innocuous at the time, and I might add that it was funny. Later I was made to realize that it was rude. I was also rude as I talked out loud with my friends during the worship service. On numerous occasions the preacher came to a dead stop in the middle of the sermon, interrupted us while we were talking, and ordered us to quiet down because we were creating a disturbance. In turn, I felt the preacher was rude as well for embarrassing us in front of everyone.

Aside from being rude, I had good study habits throughout my school years. In fact, my 4th grade teacher suggested that I skip a grade because she felt I was academically ahead of all of the other students in my grade. I can't recall why, but for some reason I did not take her advice.

When I entered junior high and high school, I finally became tall and thin, and as a result developed a higher self-esteem. I became active in school activities, clubs, band, and cheerleading. I was a contestant on the homecoming court, which was an honor and I also pledged for and became a member of a sorority. I remember during hell night, my sister cracked a raw egg on my tooth and I had to swallow it. Anyway, as time passed I became somewhat popular. I was extremely outgoing to the point of being flirtatious. I began to feel as if other females didn't like me because of the relationships I had with guys. On one occasion some females on the school bus yelled obscenities and threw oranges at me. I felt threatened and didnn't know what to expect from day to day. I can actually remember feeling frightened. I had several girls approach me ready to fight for no reason at all. In fact, I had never even spoken to or knew them. I always felt nervous and begun to dislike going to school. You would never know it now because life has made me change. On another occasion, when I was in college, someone wrote on the bathroom door that they hated me. It almost sounds like I was the bad guy. Although it hurt my feelings, in some sick way I was honored. I thought I had developed into an attractive woman, so to speak, but now when I refer back to my high school yearbook I don't know what I was thinking. I became more attractive during my college years.

As a teenager, I was easily spooked and developed a sense of extreme paranoia for indefinite prolonged periods of time after seeing terrifying movies. My fears became my obsession, and no matter how hard I tried to fight it, my overactive imagination prevailed. I remember seeing "The Amityville Horror". For months I was afraid to go upstairs to my bedroom. I imagined blood running down the hallway walls, and I was so scared that there was someone in the walk-in attic next to my bedroom. Perhaps my experiences were no different than those of others. Mine were just so extreme as I was very terrified of the paranormal.

I started dating when I was 15 years old even though my dad said I couldn't until I was 19. My first date was a double date. I wasn't attracted to my date at all, but I wanted to go out just to see what dating was like. My date had flaming red hair, not that there is anything wrong with that. My friend from high school and her date went along with us. I can remember feeling grossed out. My friend felt the same way about her date. We went to a movie that I can't remember the first thing about probably because all that I could think of was that I wanted to go home! My friend and I practically held each other's hands to avoid holding theirs and we weren't even close to being gay. After the movie, we stopped at the neighborhood Seven Eleven. As soon as our dates got out of the car to go in to the store, we locked the doors. When they returned we wouldn't let them in the car because they gave us the creeps! We couldn't stand to be with them. Oh Lord, I can still see the expressions on their faces. That is where my memory stops until we were dropped off at my yard. My girlfriend and I shouted cheers and did high kicks when they left. Oh, the stupidity of youth.

Several weeks after my first date I met my first love after a church basketball game. After several dates, he decided he would attempt to feel my boobs. I let him. When I went to bed later that evening I felt like a tramp! I felt so guilty that I went to the Lord in prayer and said, "Oh God please forgive me. I won't let him go any further." The next date we went a little further, so I had to say to my Lord, "Oh God, please forgive me" a second time. I promised Him I wouldn't let my boyfriend go any further. I prayed at the end of each date, but it did no good. I was weak like anybody else. We never did have sex however because I was afraid of getting pregnant. In the end my common sense, my conscience, and my prayers helped after all. After two years of the hell that I must have put my boyfriend through, he broke up with me. I'm sure his racing hormones had something to do with it.

I believe this phase in my life could have been the onset of my disorder. I had more than an extremely hard time adjusting to our breakup. I cried for days and couldn't function well in school.

My dad actually had to shake me in order for me to snap out of it while telling me to get a grip. I was severely depressed for several weeks, but was still not over him even during my first marriage. By this time eight years had passed. I had developed an obsession for him, but it wasn't because of love, it was because of the rejection. I couldn't handle it.

I graduated from high school back in 1980 and decided to attend a local community college because I didn't know what direction to take in life. Little did I know when I started going to college I was on the road to self-destruction.

CHAPTER 5

THE ROAD TO SELF—DESTRUCTION

During my first year of junior college I dated a guy from Jordan who transferred to a University in Ohio to study Civil Engineering. After he left I was devastated and shut myself in my bedroom for two days. My mother took me to a psychiatrist thinking that I might need medication to help me through this difficult period. Several members of my extended family had already been diagnosed with Manic-Depression and my mother thought that since it was genetic, I might be affected. It was then, at age 18, I was actually diagnosed with this same disorder. My psychiatrist prescribed lithium, which is a mood stabilizer, and within a few days I was stabilized. After a while (not recalling how long) my condition worsened. I decompensated and I began to behave recklessly.

I began wasting my time and my parents money on my education. All I wanted to do was "party." I went to parties and nightclubs with my friends several times a week. My favorite alcoholic beverage was the "Margarita," not only for it's taste but for it's potency. After consuming five or six drinks, enough to become highly intoxicated, I would have to take off my shoes because my feet would swell from the mixture of lithium and the alcohol. They would swell so badly I could barely walk much less drive in the condition I was in.

I began smoking cigarettes and using recreational drugs such as marijuana, speed and cocaine. Unlike some of my friends, I was afraid of using hallucinogenic drugs such as acid. However, I did hallucinate on marijuana once or twice. In fact, I was driving home from a friend's home and I thought I saw a river of blood flowing down the highway toward me as I was driving the car. I freaked out but still continued to use drugs for some time. I knew I wasn't supposed to drink or use drugs while taking the medication because of the harmful effects it could have had on me, but I did anyway. It seemed like the marijuana helped to temporarily relieve my depression. However, when I look back to that time in my life, it frightens me.

One night after drinking and dancing at a popular nightclub across town, I met a very nice looking guy that I became interested in. He approached me, we talked and then we took our conversation outside. I was poisoned by alcohol and apparently gave him the wrong impression that I was a little loose. By the end of the evening, we made plans to go out on a date the next day. I thought we would go to the movies or something of that nature, but instead he took me to a secluded place and sexually assaulted me. For a while it entered my mind that the date would end in a case of date rape. He forced himself on me, tried to take off my clothes, but did not succeed. I kept saying "no," but he did not want that for an answer. It wasn't until he partially ejaculated on my stomach that he stopped what he was about to do. From then on my memory escapes me, but I was pretty shaken. After some time had passed, I began believing the incident was partly my fault because I had led him on the night before, however "no means no."

While in college, I was selected to rum for the Miss RBC pageant. Although I didn't win, I still used my outward appearance to my advantage when it came to men. I lost my virginity at the age of eighteen, I relinquished my religious beliefs and I became promiscuous. I had a mixed high and low self-esteem, but having sex with men gave me a sense of self-worth. My self-esteem was defined by my outward appearance instead of who I was as a person.

Following are some incidents that I experienced while in Junior College. It is difficult for me to talk about these things, but at the same time they may prove to be of help to someone else when identifying a potential diagnosis of Bipolar Disorder. Some of the behavior may be indicative of Bipolar Disorder, of course, if additional symptoms are present.

During this time I became a thief. Several of my friends would join me at the mall and we would steal hundreds of dollars worth of clothing. We would visit all of the department stores, stuff clothes underneath our jackets and in our pocketbooks, go to the car, load up the trunk and go back for more. We finally got caught one day and were threatened that we would be arrested, but we were lucky. That was it for me. I learned my lesson and never did it again.

Shortly after this incident, I was involved in a hit and run car accident. I backed into a moving car and put a nice big dent on both their front and back doors. There was a man and his wife in the car at the time. We exchanged the auto insurance information, but somehow in all the confusion, I ended up with my own information and he ended up with his. As soon as I noticed it, I bolted like lightening resulting in a very precarious situation. It wasn't a speedy chase, but the man tried to catch up with me and failed. I didn't feel any remorse at all. I thought it was funny at the time. I was afraid of getting in trouble with my parents, never mind getting in trouble with the law. What an idiot!

I must portray myself as being a shady character at that time. At age 19 when I was going into my second year of college, I took a religion class. A friend and I cheated on the final exam at the end of the semester. Two obese girls sitting next to us from a sorority nicknamed "Psi Alpha Cows" turned us in for cheating. In that particular class almost everybody cheated because of the type of professor we had. We just got caught! We had to appear in front of the honor court of which some members were friends. I think it was the most embarrassing thing I had ever been through. The entire student body, of course, found out and I didn't want to show my face to anyone ever again. Finally, we were kicked out of college and received grades of F for the class. By that time I was a disgrace to the family.

In the above events, I used poor judgement which is highly indicative of Manic-Depression. However, it is difficult to know where to draw the line when it comes to self-destruction brought on by mental illness, self-destruction brought on by a glitch in the maturational process, or for that matter both. I believe my illness played a role in all of my actions to a degree. With that being the case, it would have been easy to let myself off the hook and not be held accountable for my actions. At the same time, when I am depressed, I feel guilty and blame myself for all the things that have happened to me. Keep in mind, many individuals may exhibit the same delinquent behaviors and are not mentally ill, but may be influenced by the dynamics of their familial system.

A year later I decided to go back to college (Virginia Commonwealth University), majored in Public Relations, and graduated in 1986. I held several jobs but either got fired or quit because of my illness. I missed a lot of days from work when I felt bad or often cried while at work. I became an unreliable employee. Three years later I became desperate, went back to college and pursued a Master's Degree in Social Work. I figured that since I had psychiatric problems, maybe I could be helpful to others with psychiatric problems. After completing the Master's program, I held several more jobs and again failed due to the stress involved. It was so discouraging to have gone this far in life and turn out to be, what I felt like, a failure! People would tell me, "You should be proud of yourself for receiving the degree" and "no one can ever take it away." How sensitively insensitive. From my standpoint that is almost an insult. What good is it if you can't use the damn thing? Again, I wasted my time, my dreams and my money.

CHAPTER 6

THE UGLY DUCKLING SYNDROME

This chapter was written at a time when I was somewhat depressed but very agitated and angry. All of my thoughts and beliefs still hold truth, though at the time they may have been exaggerated a bit. Everything is written as it was at the time and no changes have been made except for a few deletions.

I would like to share my thoughts on my reflection in the mirror; white trash, being a "bad ass" and boundary problems. After all the mistakes I had made in my life, I began to have a very low-self-image. I can remember feeling so good about myself when I was in high school. I thought I was going to be a successful person with a lot to be proud of. Then when I started self-destructing, I began to think I was a failure. Unfortunately, I still feel that way. I feel ugly inside and out and I'm often depressed. When I used to go out at night with my friends, not only was I depressed, I was angry. I can remember looking in the mirror seeing nothing but ugliness. When my mood shifted to a higher gear, I thought I was attractive, and sometimes almost beautiful. That is embarrassing to say since in reality I'm closer to average looking. I would say to myself in the mirror, "Look out Mother F-----, here I come." Obviously I was still angry inside because I knew I was so sick. Now I am older and not as attractive and thin as I used to be, which makes matters worse. As my Grandmother used to say, "There are two things you can't change----your age and the weather." Since I have so much going against me, I have nothing to offer but my appearance and my personality and both "suck" depending on my mood at the time.

My ability to meet the criteria for success has diminished. It makes me feel like a heel when I meet someone and they ask me, "What do you do, Cherie?". I have to reply, "I don't work." Then they look at me as if they expect an explanation. For some reason I always feel compelled to tell the truth as to why I don't work while at the same time feeling ashamed of the way my life has turned out. But the "killer" response to me is, "Well at least you've got your health." Spare me the old cliché. Sometimes people ask, "Do you have any children?" I just say "No, I don't." It nearly kills me knowing I can't have children much less talk about it. I think about it all the time, and it hurts to see other people with children. No, I don't feel compelled to talk about that to people.

Now that I have gotten started, I have some thoughts on "white trash.". According to my personal dictionary, "white trash" is a derogatory label predominately given to the lower socioeconomic class of people (who look and behave in certain ways) by the snobbish, judgmental, higher socioeconomic class of people (who feel more superior). Hats off to white trash! First of all, I seem to be more accepted by this so-called class of people. Second, even though I don't look the part, my behavior is indigenous to people who are labeled "white trash." Maybe I'm paranoid, but my perception is that the more elite people tend to distance themselves from me once they discover that I am Bipolar and then look down on me as if I am a freak of nature.

My first psychiatrist explained to me that I would probably mature by the age of 30. I am 45 years old now and it "ain't" happened yet. In fact, my behavior and moods have progressively gotten worse. I have become more angry and bitter as I've gotten older. When I'm agitated, I make my own enemies. I am extremely confrontational with anyone who may stand in my way at the wrong place and the wrong time. I become a "bad ass" and sometimes cause irrefutable damage amongst my peers. Life has made me this way.

Now I would like to share my thoughts about boundary problems. I have been told by many people that I have a boundary problem. It is true to a degree. A portion of my problem may be due to my personality deficits, but part of it is due to my illness. I tend to blurt out things right off the top of my head without filtering out what I should say. Back in 1984 I was interviewed by a sergeant in the Army for a job. I got the job but was told he hired me for my pretty legs. I was flattered. Now, do you consider him to have a boundary problem? Although he didn't embarrass me, he may have embarrassed or offended someone else. So when is it considered a boundary problem?

I started seeing a psychiatrist back in 1993 and on my first visit he told me I was a "9" on a scale of "1 to 10." I had dreams of having sex with him following that incident and I expressed that to him. Who had the boundary problem? Did the psychiatrist for saying what he said? Or did I have a boundary problem because I told him I had dreams of having sex with him? Shouldn't a patient tell the psychiatrist everything so that he or she can get adequate treatment? In my opinion, boundary problems are relative to the circumstances presented. Why did I get "boundary problem" plastered on my forehead?

CHAPTER 7

THE BACK—UP SYSTEM

Does the saying, "once a cheater, always a cheater" hold truth? In some cases I'm sure it's possible. During both of my previous marriages, infidelity became an issue and a reason for divorce. Even though cheating is cheating, with no excuses, there are reasons which lead to this type of unacceptable behavior. In my particular case, I call it "The Back-up System."

I married for the first time when I was 26 years old, two years out of college, March 1988 to a man I met at a local nightclub. He actually worked there (a second job) as a bouncer while balancing a successful career as well. Not only was he tall, dark, handsome and very well built, he was part French. He was born and raised during part of his childhood in Paris and spoke the language fluently, which was very appealing to me. He was 11 years older than me, but at the time it didn't matter. It wasn't until we actually married that the age difference worked against us. He became a father figure to me which led to an unhealthy relationship. He was a wonderful man in so many ways and I loved him, but I loved him in the wrong way. When I look back, I don't know what I was thinking when I married him. In fact, I don't know why he married me. He had told me he didn't want to get married at the beginning of our relationship. I guess he had his reservations because he had been married before, and he had always told me that if we got married, I would leave him for a younger man. The night we got married I dreaded making love to him because, although he had a gorgeous body, sex with him felt like incest. Regardless, I had to force myself to perform.

Before and during the course of our marriage, I went through a period in my life where I was very unstable. I became confused and violent. I had very rapid mood swings and would get upset over the least little thing. I can remember on one occasion when we had a dispute, he stopped talking to me and began to give me the "silent treatment". While I continued arguing, he decided to take a shower. While he was showering I became so furious that I went into the bathroom and ripped the shower curtain down as he stood there soaking wet. At times I would also throw things at him, run into the bedroom and lock the door.

We used to go bike riding quite often. Occasionally he would ride in front of me and I would very quietly, without him knowing, turn around and go back home. He would eventually come home upset realizing I wasn't behind him and would question what was wrong with me. Besides being treated for Bipolar Disorder, I didn't have an answer. The only thing I knew was that I was mentally sick.

My husband put me through graduate school and about the same time I became an aerobics instructor at a fitness center. I gained a lot of confidence in myself, perhaps too much. I wasn't searching for a relationship while I was married. In fact, I never dreamed of it.

Then it happened out of nowhere! I became attracted to this really cute guy around my age who participated in my aerobics class. He had blonde curly hair and beautiful blue eyes, not to mention he was in great shape. He was a successful computer programmer and made a good living. We began flirting with each other, and it became very noticeable to others, especially to those who knew I was married. We began sneaking around to see each other and within one to two months we were in love. I had plans to leave my husband and plans to marry this man; but first I had to make sure he wanted to marry me as well. That was my agenda. After finding out that he wanted to marry me and could take care of me financially, emotionally and intimately, the beginning of "The Back-up System" came into fruition. I would not have been able to leave my first husband on my own. I had to have someone as a backup to take care of me. My sister tried to convince me to stop what I was doing, but I wouldn't listen. After two months of unfaithfulness to my husband, I took a gamble and moved in with my future husband to be. The whole affair from beginning to end happened so quickly I couldn't even think about what I was doing. It was as if I were in a dream which later would become a real emotional nightmare (which I deserved).

One year later (1991) my divorce was final and I married my second husband in 1992. I was married to my first husband a total of three years. I knew what I had done was wrong, but I couldn't control my feelings. I must be careful to say that manic-depressives often operate off of feelings rather than logic. At least that is the way I have always operated. I felt guilty and depressed about what I had done to my first husband because I still cared for him a great deal. I obsessed over it and called him on many occasions to apologize for what I had done. The guilt ate me alive and lasted my entire second marriage (7 years).

I believe my second husband was attracted to me in the beginning because it appeared as though I was going to be a very successful person because I had obtained a Master's Degree. I also believe he had very high expectations of me that I eventually could not meet. Then it all fell apart when I was placed on disability. I guess you could say "that was the straw that broke the camel's back." Before I started collecting disability, I held several jobs that didn't work out. They were too stressful for me, therefore I quit working or got fired because each time I began to decompensate. I had held close to 30 jobs so far in my life and that was a sure sign that something was wrong.

We had a very lovely home that we had to quickly sell since I wasn't bringing in enough income from disability. I'm sure that disappointed my husband greatly. I don't have any definite answers because my husband would not communicate his true feelings to me.

Before we got married, his mother almost immediately went to the library to research Manic-Depression. I don't know how she learned of my condition. However, I do have an idea. She tried to persuade her son not to marry me. Although his mother had a lot of influence on him, he married me anyway. It was obvious she didn't approve of me, but she managed to develop a superficial relationship with me for our own good.

After two or three years of marriage, my husband began to sexually neglect me. After months of neglect, I began to cry and beg for intimacy. I began to feel as though I was unattractive. We spoke with my psychiatrist about it, but my husband always gave some lame excuse that he was too tired to have sex. The breakdown in communication and the neglect lasted the remaining years of our marriage.

During the course of our marriage, I had to be hospitalized because I was unstable and needed a medication adjustment. I had to rely on my mother and sister to take me to the hospital because my husband didn't want to. In retrospect, I think my husband was probably embarrassed because of me. Needless to say after seven years of marriage, most of which I was neglected, I became very unstable.

My parents had owned an art and crafts store during the last three years of my second marriage. One day a very fine-looking gentleman came in to visit. I had known him in high school but we hadn't seen each other in years. He told me that he was living with his older girlfriend, but was very unhappy. He also said that he had been in a very serious car accident which almost took his life a few years back and added that his girlfriend helped nurse him back to health. He indicated that he felt sort of obligated to her, but wanted to get out of the relationship. I told him I was unhappily married, but still married. He gave me his card and told me to call him if I was interested in seeing him.

The last few years my husband and I were together, he mentioned that he didn't want any children; however, I did. I felt deep inside that he didn't want any because he wasn't happy with me. Whether I wanted to admit it or not, our marriage was in trouble. I approached him the next morning and asked him what he would choose: one, for us to have a family, or two, for me to leave? He replied, "leave." That morning I went to work at my parents' store in tears. I knew I needed to find a "back-up system" fast! I knew our marriage was headed for destruction! I thought about it, picked up the phone and called that fine-looking man that left me his card. We met that same day. Again, I couldn't walk out of a marriage without someone lined up to take care of me financially, emotionally and intimately. We talked and each time we saw each other we became closer and closer. He told me that he gave his girlfriend, who lived with him, 90 days to move out and find a place to live. I was led to believe that they split up. Again, I was in the middle of an extra-marital affair, but in a sense with good reason. Actually, there is really no good reason, but in my world it was called survival.

One afternoon I met my boyfriend for lunch at a park. He had one of his co-workers drop him off. I felt very seductive that day, so I wore a black teddy underneath my clothing. Later I seduced him into having sex with me in the woods. Following our sexual encounter, I distinctly remember a man jogging toward us through the park and then he passed us. He was wearing a light blue shirt and a pair of blue jeans. While I was unsuccessfully putting my clothes back on, he began making his way back toward us. He kept staring at me as he passed by. I was still naked but was in a crunched position. After he passed us we finally got our clothes back on and I made my way back to my car while my boyfriend left with his co-worker. I could have sworn the man was hiding in the woods watching our every move. We left the premises and I drove home. I didn't notice anyone following me. My husband was waiting for me to get home so we could go look at cars and possibly purchase one. When I pulled in the driveway, out of nowhere the man from the park approached me at my car door before I even had a chance to open it. I was frantic! The man said, "You have a nice tan." He gave me his card with his name and number on it. He said, "Call me when you are ready to be with me." I said very softly with a trembling voice, "alright" just so he would hurry up and leave. Then he said, "I know you are married." He left and I thought I would have a heart attack! I felt like I was being blackmailed! He had to have illegally found out my address because when I arrived at my home, he was already there waiting for me. How did he know I was married? Did my husband see us outside? Would I get caught in the act? What kind of lie would I have to come up with to cover my tracks? I went inside my home overwhelmed with trepidation. I felt so much anxiety I thought I was going to lose control. I knew I wanted to end my marriage, but not this way! When I walked into the living room, my husband was sitting in the chair next to the window that overlooked the driveway. I could barely look him in the eyes. I felt myself falling apart. I knew it was the end. He asked me, "Are you ready to go look at cars?" Thank God. We drove separately to the dealership, so I called my boyfriend on my cell phone and told him what had happened. I gave him my stalker's name and number, and his co-worker called him and threatened him. I never heard from this man again.

My husband and I decided to separate in September of 1999. I moved in with my aunt who lived in very close proximity to my boyfriend. He never wanted me to call his home because his ex-girlfriend always got the messages and they had caller ID. One afternoon he wanted me to go to the doctor's office with him. He took off early that day, so I felt it was safe to call him. He wasn't home yet so I left a message on his answering machine. I assumed that when he got home he would retrieve the message and return the call. Incidentally, while his ex-girlfriend was at work she called home and retrieved the message before he did. He became frantic and began to actually panic. I didn't understand since they had supposedly split up. That should have been a red flag to me, but I always gave him the benefit of the doubt. His ex-girlfriend called my parents' business and asked to speak to me, however I wasn't there. My parents were oblivious to what was going on and gave her my aunt's telephone number in order for her to reach me. She contacted me and confronted me about my relationship with "our" boyfriend since he made himself a boyfriend to both of us. She asked me to come to their house and force him to choose between the two of us. He had been lying to me all along. They had never split up!

He wasn't home at the time, but somehow we tracked him down at a friend's house. He was sitting in the garage extremely intoxicated. You could tell from the look on his face he was troubled about his situation. The three of us went back to his or her home, who knew by this time. They began arguing outside while the neighbors came out and observed one by one. He became violent and broke their flag pole over his knee. I began to get nervous. I asked that the three of us take our problem inside. We went in and they continued to argue. He admitted to her that he was seeing me. He told her he loved her but was not "in love" with her and that I could have children while she couldn't. As the argument escalated, he headed for the refrigerator, took out a container and popped himself over the head hard enough to make himself bleed. He then went upstairs to get a gun. His "other" girlfriend called 911 and reported him to the police. She tried to convince me to go outside with her to get away from him as he was a danger to himself and possibly to others. However, I stayed inside. He held the gun to his head and threatened to kill himself. I screamed, "No!" I was petrified. I tried to convince him to put the gun down because I loved him (at least I thought I did). The Sheriff arrived with two other officers. They charged him with a felony and arrested him. I followed him to the jail, and after we arrived he looked at me in desperation and motioned for us to remain together. I motioned back that I would stay with him. I never heard from him again. I found out later through a mutual acquaintance that he was going to marry his girlfriend that he wasn't "in love" with in a matter of days. After I heard the shocking news, I went over to a friend's house, called my husband at home and begged him to take me back. He refused. As a result, my "Back-up System" failed me and I had no one to care for me.

CHAPTER 8

FLIRTING WITH DEATH

I NEVER KNEW I would be the type of person to attempt suicide. It is hard for me to believe it, yet once you've tried it, it gets easier each time.

The first time I flirted with death was when my second husband would not take me back after my affair. He wouldn't have taken me back regardless because he wasn't romantically attracted to me anymore and my affair was his excuse to get out of our marriage.

After I had called my husband to take me back and he refused, I got in my car and raced over to our home driving around 60mph in a 35mph speed zone. I had all of my medication with me so I began popping pills left and right. I was driving very wrecklessly passing cars while crossing over the double line potentially causing a head on collision. I was extremely desperate, depressed and agitated. After I left my friend's home, she had apparently called my mother to tell her where I was headed and also told her of the condition that I was in. When I finally pulled in the driveway, I realized my mother was there. I pushed the back door open and threw a can of Pepsi across the room at the kitchen cabinets. I said to my husband, "Are you f——---- happy now? I've taken an overdose, and now I'm going to die like you probably want me to!"

I didn't know what I was saying or doing by that time. My mom called 911 and the police, followed by an ambulance, arrived a few minutes later. The paramedics took me to the hospital where I had my stomach pumped. After I was released from the hospital, my mother took me to a psychiatric hospital where I could get the proper care. I was so out of control I was beating on the walls and screaming obscenities at the staff to give me my clothes. They threatened to put me in restraints if I didn't calm down and decided to give me medication to sedate me. I stayed in the hospital for one week, and my husband didn't call or visit the entire time I was there.

I remember my preacher coming to visit me and I told him, of all people, that I was a very sexual person and that I needed to have a man in my life. He replied, "I know you are. You will find someone soon." Sure enough while I was there I met a patient on the unit that was fairly attractive. I don't know why he was there, but we "hooked up." Although it was delayed, "the backup system" came to fruition again, only this time I was taking desperate measures to have a relationship with someone as unstable as I. My new friend and I had pleasurable conversation with one another and began to really appreciate each other. We were so sexually attracted to each other that we would sneak into the laundry room in the hospital while another patient was on guard duty for us. We became very familiar with each other, to put it nicely. We made plans to see each other on a regular basis after discharge from the hospital. However, the next morning he was arrested for failing to pay child support. I never heard from him again.

When I was discharged from the hospital, I moved back in with my parents so they could keep an eye on me. I spent a lot of time in bed as I was depressed and did not want to get up, much less socialize with anyone. In the meantime my husband finally admitted to me in front of a therapist on a one time visit that he was not romantically attracted to me (since he didn't have the guts to tell me when we were alone). Wow! What a blow to the ego! It wasn't until later that I realized he had scarred me for life!

I lost any self-esteem I had ever had. In addition to feeling unattractive, I ruminated over not being able to make it on my own since I received such a ridiculous small amount of money for disability. I thought I would have to live with my parents from then on because I knew I wouldn't be able to find someone to love me with my condition much less support me financially. It wasn't a week later that I went on a man hunt. I met three different guys over a three-week period, all of whom were married and all with whom I committed adultery. It was a though I was on a sexual rampage. By this time I was self-destructing again at a very rapid pace. I was so desperate to have a man in my life at any cost.

A couple of weeks later I went on a date with a friend to a karaoke bar. Unfortunately I made a wrong move by going with him because he liked me for more than a friend. We sat at the bar and ordered drinks. There was a very mysterious looking guy sitting beside me on my left with dark hair and dark eyes. I didn't consider my date's feelings and I began talking to this guy. I noticed my date was becoming slightly annoyed with me so I tried to divide my attention equally between them. How nice of me. My date went to the restroom and while he was gone we exchanged telephone numbers. Somehow my date got back from the restroom sooner than anticipated, and caught on to what we were doing. I thought, gosh this is really rude of me. My date took me home and never spoke to me again. However, my mystery man called me and asked me out for a date for the next evening.

The next evening we had plans to go to a movie, however, we had some time to spare so he took me over to his place. He showed me books on Borderline Personality Disorder, which he had been diagnosed by a therapist. He also showed me books on Christianity. He was a devout Christian and attended bible study regularly. He was separated from his wife and was having a hard time dealing with it. He needed a friend and I was the chosen one for the time being. I was a bad choice. I was very confused at the time. I felt so sexually neglected by my ex-husband that I still thought something was wrong with me. So, I put it to the test. I felt as though there was something evil within me, almost as if I had a demon in me. I knew that he didn't want to commit adultery, but it didn't matter to me. I thought to myself, "I'll win you over Jesus Christ." How could I have had those thoughts since I was a good Christian as well. So, I went into his bathroom and removed all of my clothing except for my black panties and black bra. I walked out of the bathroom with an overload of confidence. I seduced him and he did not resist me. It wasn't until after we engaged in carnal pleasures that I had satisfied my curiosity as to whether I was desirable or not.

It was then that I realized why I had become promiscuous again. I couldn't handle the rejection from my second marriage. I realized it wasn't me. There had to be something more to it than my ex-husband not being romantically attracted to me. The next morning my date from the night before called and apologized for everything that happened the night before. He said he was weak and we should never allow ourselves to get in that situation again.

I went over to his apartment to watch a football game the next day. I still had in mind, "I'll win you over Jesus Christ," but I didn't win this time. The following Sunday I went to church and the evil inside of me immediately ceased. There might not have been an actual demon, but it was definitely Satan controlling my mind and thoughts at the time. After church, I felt spiritually cleansed. I called him up and told him everything that I had been thinking and doing to get him to sleep with me and apologized. We decided never to see each other again. I think he went back to his wife.

About one month later, while I was still on a man hunt, I went into a dive bar to get tickets to a concert for a friend and myself. I had no intentions of meeting anyone, especially in a place like that. I was approached by a guy who looked a little rough around the edges, but very appealing to me. Of all things, I was attracted to his sexy mustache. He approached me and said, "Hey beautiful lady. Would you like to play some pool and drink a beer?" I agreed not really wanting to, but it was an opportunity to meet someone while on my man hunt.

We started dating and at first I didn't even really like him but, I guess, as usual I had to have someone in my life. Later, however, I fell hard for him.

The relationship became unhealthy and again I began to self-destruct. We consumed a lot of alcohol on a routine basis over a six-month period. I became quite unstable due to the mixture of alcohol and my medication. He was eight years younger than me and did not have his head in the same place I did. I wanted to settle down but he didn't at the time. He was a "dead beat dad," had four children by three different women and was concerned I would trap him with another child. However, he had much deeper issues. He was living with his grandmother at the time.

After several months of dating, he began to cheat on me, but I refused to see the signs. Our relationship had become based on lies and deceit. He wanted out of our relationship, but I didn't. Instead of letting him go, he became an obsession to me probably because I wanted something I couldn't have. I was beginning to feel hopeless and extremely depressed. One night I finally took a massive overdose of pills when he pulled a weekend disappearing act on me. I laid in his bed and took at least 40 pills of all different types. I left a suicide note to my parents and to him as well. After I took the pills I asked God to please take me into his kingdom and to please forgive me for what I was doing. I told God I just couldn't go on any longer and I had nothing to live for anymore. That was the last thing I remembered until the next morning at 8:00 a.m. sharp. It was as if I hadn't even tried to kill myself. I looked on the comforter and the floor and there was powder all over the place. God had saved me. There were no signs of vomit, only plain long powder. Now I can look back at it as a miracle. It wasn't my time to go.

I quietly left his grandmother's trailer without anyone knowing. I had driven my father's truck at the time. I drove off and within a few minutes I wrecked it while I was on the way home. I had slammed into the guard rail in my attempt to get on the interstate. I felt completely numb and in a state of shock from the overdose the night before and didn't realize I had done any damage to the vehicle. However, my father noticed it and became very upset wondering how in the world it happened. He knew I was in really bad shape and wasn't too hard on me.

Recently I watched a television program which actually showed a way to kill yourself. If I had seen it prior to my attempt, I might have done it the way it was shown. My boyfriend and I broke up a couple of months later. I admitted myself to the hospital because I couldn't cope with the loss , and I new I needed to get control of my life again. I had to do this without being involved in a relationship. One of the psychiatrists in the hospital told me there was nothing they could do for me. I came back home to stay with my parents in such a deep depression I didn't know what to do. Every time I walked by the counter in the utility room I would look at the bottle of pesticide laying on top and seriously contemplate using that as my way out. I wrote suicide notes to all of my family members but hid them until I was ready to take my life. I never went out of the house. All I did was sleep and lay on the couch and watch TV. Again I knew deep inside I would never meet anyone again who would love me.

As the days passed I began to feel a little bit better, and I got the idea in my head to call a dating service. I couldn't believe the type of people with the same idea. One couple wanted to have a Menage a' trois. Another man said he wanted his date to dress in drag. Most of the people were up front about wanting to have sexual experiences. I knew this wasn't the route I wanted to take. I wanted a relationship. I knew I had to do something else to meet a nice person, but I didn't know what.

People would sometimes say to me, "Why do you always have to have a man in your life?" My only answer is "A man makes me complete." I'm sure it goes a lot deeper than that, but I didn't want to take the time for therapy to find out. At that point in my life I was at "rock bottom" because I knew I was alive and alone and had to face the world.

CHAPTER 9

FINDING MR. RIGHT

It was a hot summer day in June of 2000. I had been depressed for two months and did nothing but seclude myself from everybody and everything around me. I finally forced myself to go out to a social event presented by the City of Petersburg at the Ironworks. It was an outdoor event held every Thursday evening. A certain type of people attend this event. Those who like to drink beer, listen to a band, dance and socialize with one another. I didn't look forward to going to this function because it's really not my cup of tea. Besides, depression kills a good time. However, I decided to go anyway. I went alone because all of my friends were all married, had children and were at different stages in their lives. When I got there I almost dreaded walking in the entrance gate, so I tried hard not to think about it. In so many instances, things aren't as bad as they seem. However, I knew that I needed an attitude adjustment immediately if I had any intention of meeting somebody. So I marched over to the beer wagon, got myself a beer, guzzled it down, got myself another, guzzled it down and started working on getting "happy." After about forty-five minutes of drinking more beer and scoping out the scene, I saw a "hot-looking guy" standing alone across the party zone. I knew I had to use the aggressive part of my personality, put a smile on my face (even if it was fake) and introduce myself to him. After I approached him, my fake smile turned into a big fat genuine smile that wouldn't quit. We began dating and 10 weeks later we were married. We knew we got married fast according to society's standards and that people would talk, but we didn't care. We have been married for eight years and we couldn't be happier. The funny thing is I never really knew who I was or who I could be until I met him. I have never had anyone tell me that he/she would like to be me for a while just to feel what I feel. But my husband, after eight years of living with a Manic-Depressive, told me that he would like to be me for a while just to know how I feel. Now that's true love and I actually felt honored. I mean, who would actually want to be me?

My husband's name is John and it's the only name I feel I can mention in this book. Not only was John the "underdog" in his family, it was made clear to him that he was.

When he speaks of his upbringing, it is heartbreaking to hear. He is the youngest of 13 children. All of his siblings are half brothers and sisters except for one sister who is very close to him. His mother had six children by her husband then had John and his sister by her lover who lived in the same house. His father had five children from another relationship. His mother had physical and emotional problems most of the time, so his father mainly cared for John and his sister while she stayed in bed. His father always told him he wouldn't amount to anything.

Many times the children had to sleep in their coats at night in order to stay warm. In one particular house he lived in, they had to resort to an "out-house" for bathroom purposes. As a result, John felt a little embarrassed to have friends come to visit him. He jokes and compares his previous homes to that of the TV sitcom, "Sanford & Son," but only worse. He was raised as a Catholic and attended a Catholic school with children that were from wealthy families. Many times he got his clothing from the school's "lost and found." On several occasions he remembered students saying that the clothes he had on belonged to them. John would reply, "Not no more, it's mine now." I think he handled that well considering the embarrassment he suffered. In later years John worked very hard and beat his odds for success through leadership and financial prosperity in his career.

His humble upbringing and my mental illness allow us to relate to one another on a level that I have never experienced with anyone else. I believe since his mother had emotional problems, he became accustomed to dealing with and understanding my mental illness. Our love for each other extends to the fullest, and I definitely believe the two of us were brought together by God.

As the years have passed John has witnessed a few serious Manic-Depressive episodes. Once I was taking Seroquel which caused a tremendous weight gain of 60 lbs. I asked my psychiatrist to please take me off of this medication and replace it with another drug that didn't cause weight gain. I was prescribed the new medication and lost ten lbs. in three days, but unfortunately, it wasn't worth it. I became very manic and agitated for a number days. I caused an argument with some of John's family members. I mean these were people that meant a great deal to me. I could have caused irrefutable damage to my relationship with them. I was lucky they were nice enough to forgive me. During this episode I decided to count the number of pills I was taking daily. I was alarmed when I realized I was swallowing 34 pills each day. I immediately got back on the original medications and I eventually returned to my baseline mood.

CHAPTER 10

THE MADNESS WITHIN

All of the hardships, turmoil and frustrations I've experienced in my life have caused me to feel anger toward myself. It is as though I take the blame for my unfortunate condition. As a result, I have had impulsive feelings to inflict pain on myself. For example, I have impulsive thoughts to burn myself with cigarettes, stab myself in the stomach with a knife, or slice my wrists for self-punishment because of the frustration and hatred I feel toward myself.

The following episode took place on July 16, 2005. I had been feeling horribly depressed for the last several days. I began to feel like I might have to admit myself to a hospital because I could barely function. I was in the process of receiving treatment from a new psychiatrist at the local

Community Services Board, however, I was in between doctors and couldn't be seen by a new doctor for approximately one month. I was in deep trouble. Although I wasn't supposed to, I felt I had no choice but to monitor my own illness and make any medication adjustments if needed until I could get some help. I was on my own and in a slump. As the days passed, I became worse. I actually thought I was losing my mind but I didn't want to go to the dreaded hospital. I began to feel confused and as though I was in and out of reality. In fact I may have been entering into a state of psychosis. I started questioning God's existence because no matter how hard or how much I prayed, he wouldn't help me. I begged him for his mercy and asked that he would deliver me from my depression, but he wouldn't. I started decompensating at a rapid pace. It was the scariest and strangest episode I had ever had and hopefully the last of it's kind. My husband and I laid in bed that morning and we began to have a very deep discussion about God. As much as I had believed in God and had faith all of my life, it was as if I had been struck by a bolt of lightening and began to deny God's existence. I had always put so much energy in prayer and all of a sudden I went into a state of disbelief. A few minutes later I began having thoughts of slicing my wrists because the anger within me was so intense. I cuddled up to my husband as tight as I possibly could feeling desperate as hell. I was becoming more confused and miserable. Following our conversation I had a strange sexual encounter with my husband. It was so intense on my part that I felt like it was going to be my last intimate experience with him. I was so frightened I felt as though I had lost my sanity and was losing touch with reality. I compared myself with the character Glen Close played opposite Michael Douglas in the movie, "Fatal Attraction." She (Close) was so desperate and psychotic that she sliced her wrists over the married man (Douglas) she was having an affair with when he began rejecting her. Although I had never sliced my wrists before, I felt the sickness and the intense desperation she experienced. By this time John had fallen back to sleep, so I began praying again hoping God was really there. I looked at the wall and silently asked Jesus to appear before me. Again I began to exhaust all of my energy in praying. Then I decided why pray when God is going to do what he wants, when he wants, and on his own terms. I felt so guilty that I had actually denied God's existence earlier and I was scared I would be punished. I finally took some medicine to calm down and the sick and desperate feeling subsided. The next day I started sawing on my wrist but never drew blood. I stopped because it was so painful. I still didn't see a doctor for days, so I took it upon myself to adjust my own medication and eventually became stabilized.

The next episode was taken from a recording over two years before the previous one on March 11, 2003. Even though I didn't necessarily want to inflict pain on myself during this episode, I still felt the madness inside but I tried to do something positive with my feelings.

"I feel trapped. I want to die, but I want to stay alive because I love my husband so much. I just can't hurt him. So where does that leave me? I'm in total misery. It's just not fair to me. I don't want to want to die. I actually punish myself by living. If I had a job or a career that kept me going, or if I had children to live for I would feel different. My life revolves completely around John and that is what my happiness is based on. Do you know what it is like to only live for somebody else and not value your own life? I'm not living for me. I've lost my identity. I'm living for somebody else. Do you know how that feels? I'm keeping myself alive for somebody else because I don't want to hurt him and because I love him. I don't even have a life.

As I've gotten older, my illness has progressively gotten worse. It is like I live in complete darkness and I can't see which way to turn in life. I often ask God, "Is there a purpose in life for me besides living for my husband?" There has to be something more to bring me happiness. So I did a little soul-searching and decided to form a support group for people suffering Depressive and Manic-Depressive illness. I facilitated the group with the help of my mother who is also Bipolar. The first session was very encouraging. Over a dozen people attended the meeting. I thought I had finally found my purpose in life—helping individuals who suffer from the illness.

During one group session I discussed the do's and don'ts of surviving the illness. However, while serving as a role model, I was hiding something from the group that was disturbing. I was living a double life. I was binge drinking which is a definite faux pas when taking medication. I would get so drunk, sometimes I would fall face down on the floor and embarrass my husband who would have to pick me up. Getting drunk was my way of coping with my depression. I could have created a very dangerous scenario by mixing a lot of alcohol with my medication. I can recall when there was a tornado warning in the area in which my parents lived. While I was drunk, my parents lives could have been in danger. I called them to let them know of the tornado, but they had already taken cover. All I could picture was something terrible happening to them. I went on a serious guilt trip after that and eventually stopped drinking because again I was leading a double life, preaching one thing and doing another.

As time went on, the group started to diminish to the to the point where I didn't want to facilitate it anymore so I let my mother take over. I gave it up because I was tired of it which made it easy for me to quit. That was no surprise for me to be a quitter. I felt it was another failure on my list of failures. I became very angry and discouraged with God because I thought the group might have been my purpose in life when actually it wasn't. So what now? I must continue to search for my purpose.

It is extremely important for individuals with the illness to have a support system whether it be family, friends or a group to vent your feelings and know you are not alone. I have a great support system, but I still go through periods when I feel so cumbersome. I turn to God to help me make it through each day. I turn to my friends for support and my family who provide me with empathy, encouragement and unconditional love, especially my husband who has to live with me on a daily basis. Bless his heart. He also lends me a listening ear, provides support, has patience and shows love.

CHAPTER 11

DOCTOR DO—LITTLE

I can't emphasize how important it is to find a good psychiatrist and not a quack to deliver you from your problems. At this point I have seen 15 different psychiatrists and only four have been worth a hoot. It is difficult to find a shrink who is competent and not arrogant at the same time. Don't get me wrong, I'm sure most psychiatrists are experts at what they do. I've just had some bad experiences.

Pharmacology is of main importance and proper treatment is crucial. Psychological treatment should also be utilized for coping strategies. Remember this for your first session with your doctor.

I want to focus on all of the Doctor Do-Littles that I have been exposed to over the last several years. Maybe it will help you in selecting who you want to be in charge of your mental well being.

One of my first psychiatrists decided to hospitalize me because I was depressed. However, it wasn't so severe that I was suicidal. It was the first time I had ever been admitted to a psychiatric facility. In this particular hospital there were strange looking people, some like zombies just pacing the floors. It frightened me so much that an hour later I called My husband (2nd) to come and pick me up. I gently broke the news to my psychiatrist that I was scared to be there and that I was going to return home. I asked if I could be treated on an outpatient basis. He looked at me with extreme arrogance and abruptly said, "You're fired," as if he were Donald Trump. He didn't want to continue treating me as his patient because I didn't comply with his psychiatric advice. Okay, that may have been my fault, but through most of my experiences the psychiatrist would usually be willing to treat me on an outpatient basis. If I had been experiencing suicidal thoughts, that would have been a different case. I ended up going to this same psychiatrist years later but he didn't remember me. I told him that when I got my monthly menstrual cycle I become very depressed and experience suicidal ideation. I asked him what should I do? He told me to "go hide in a closet" as he laughed. He never gave me a straight answer or recommendation to help alleviate the problem. He was leaving his practice the next week and was moving out of state. I guess he felt like "what the hell, I'll never see her again."

Another psychiatrist made the accusation that I had been using illegal drugs. The receptionist told the doctor my eyes were bloodshot and I appeared to be on drugs when in reality I had been crying prior to my appointment. It went on my medical record. Naturally I became upset and stopped seeing this psychiatrist as I was highly insulted.

A third psychiatrist tried to hypnotize me on my very first visit with him and diagnosed me as having anger problems instead of Bipolar Disorder. He never hypnotized me because I was faking. I just wanted to see what the doctor would do and say. How can he diagnose me if he doesn't know whether I'm "under" or not.

A fourth doctor tried to gradually take me off my medication to see how I would function. I ended up in the hospital. He didn't know which drugs to put me back on until my father made the suggestion to put me back on Lithium. The doctor then asked my father, "Do you think we should do this?" He obviously wasn't confident in himself as a physician.

On another occasion I was extremely agitated so I called my psychiatrist. He wasn't in his office. The receptionist transferred the call to another psychiatrist in the group. When he answered the phone, I told him I was very agitated and he replied, "You're interrupting my session. You're on too many medications and there is nothing I can do for you." Did he want to get off the hook or what? He just left me hanging. I ended up taking an overdose of Xanax to calm down. No harm was done as I just took a long nap. Regardless, that wasn't a wise thing to do.

Finally on another occasion, I called my psychiatrist (same one as above) again because I was too manic. The receptionist told me to get busy and paint the walls red. That wasn't a funny joke. Some patients in a manic state would have taken her advice. This same psychiatrist provided me with free samples of medications I could not afford to buy. After months of giving me these medications, he changed his mind and said, "I'm not a pharmacist. He was just being an ass!

Again, this same psychiatrist wanted to give me ECT (Electro-Convulsive Therapy) better known as electric shock treatment used as a last resort on patients who do not improve with any medicine. He was ready to proceed with the test without checking my blood levels. I was admitted into the hospital and a nurse tested my Lithium level which was too low and explained my depression. ECT can cause memory loss and it's not the safest procedure in treating patients. In the end I did not receive ETC thanks to the nurse.

Now you may understand the meaning of this chapter entitled Doctor Do-Little. Be very skeptical when searching for a satisfactory psychiatrist. In my experience, most of the psychiatrists I've seen are very arrogant, so you may have to overlook the attitude.

CHAPTER 12

MY PURPOSE IN LIFE

During the course of writing this book, from November 2002 to January 2009, I was in search for my purpose in life. Before when I felt there was no purpose I often envied those who had found theirs. There are so many negative components that are associated with Bipolar Disorder , it was extremely difficult for me to identify mine because of the way my illness manifested itself through the years. My mixed rapid mood swings (highs and lows occurring simultaneously) served as a deterrent from ever feeling stable long enough for contentment. It wasn't until recently when my psychiatrist prescribed a group of medicines for me that worked successfully and I became more stable. However, a more important factor had played a role in my stability and my new-found happiness.

It all began one afternoon in September of 2007. I had lunch with my mother at a local restaurant and we began talking about some of our Christian beliefs. A gentleman sitting close by must have heard what we were discussing and made a comment about how close the 2nd coming of Christ may be (Christian belief based on biblical information). This man filled my head with information that caused me to become extremely excited. When my mother and I left the restaurant and returned to her car, I expressed a huge sigh of relief. As tears began to flow down my fact I explained to my mother that if the 2nd coming of Christ is near, there is a good chance I may not have to suffer thrugh any deaths in my family. I immediately thought to myself, "maybe I won't have to take my own life"? This thought led to my second thought of how pathetic I was to still feel this way. Again, I was basing my life on whether my husband out lived me or not. Unfortunately, I haven't made any improvement in that area. I still do not live for myself! I felt that the 2nd coming is my one and only ticket out and my hope to hang on to life. I began praying harder than I ever had before. I also started studying the Bible which provided me with a sense of peace that I had never really known. In fact, praying and reading the Bible helped me change my life.

I realize that when the end of time actually occurs, (whenever that might be) all Christians including myself will ascend into heaven thus take away any misery I have on earth. There will be no more sickness or sadness thereby releasing me from my relentless pain.

Before I became closer to God, when I was extremely depressed, I wondered if God was punishing me just to see how much pain I could handle before I finally decided to end my life. After studying the scriptures, I began to see that this was not the case. In fact it was the opposite. My faith in Jesus Christ has led me to a life of more happiness and an overall increased stability. My attitude is much more positive and I feel very blessed. At forty-five years old I began to know and become closer to Jesus. I have even experienced several miracles through persistent faith and prayer.

Now I know my purpose in life is to worship Jesus Christ and witness to others by sharing my own experiences in life, and by sharing my knowledge, wisdom and faith with others.

I never felt happy without feeling sad at the same time, but having the Holy Spirit within me has allowed me to experience both emotions separately. That is so amazing to me.

I never thought I would feel this way, but since I have developed a close relationship with God I know I would choose to have my physical and mental illnesses and be close to Him rather than not have the illnesses and <u>not</u> have God. My illnesses brought me to God in the first place. My desperation has humbled me and keeps me close to the only real One that can help me.

Bibliography

Kaplan, Harold I, M.D., Sadock, Genjamin J., M.D. Synopsis of Psychitry, Behavioral Sciences/ Clinical Psychiatry, 3 ed.,Baltimore Maryland, 1998